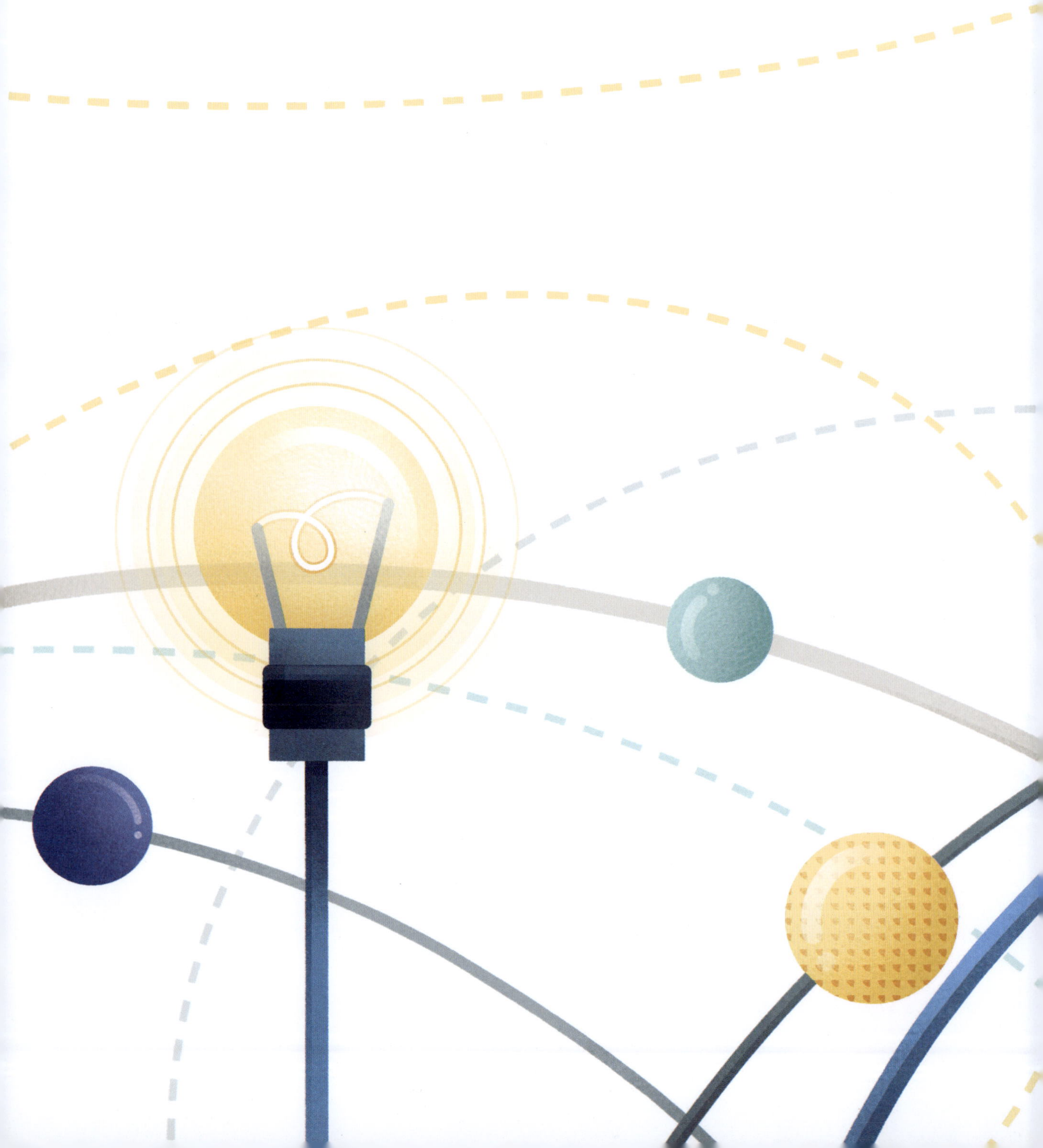

WS Kids
WHITE STAR KIDS

Electricity and Magnetism

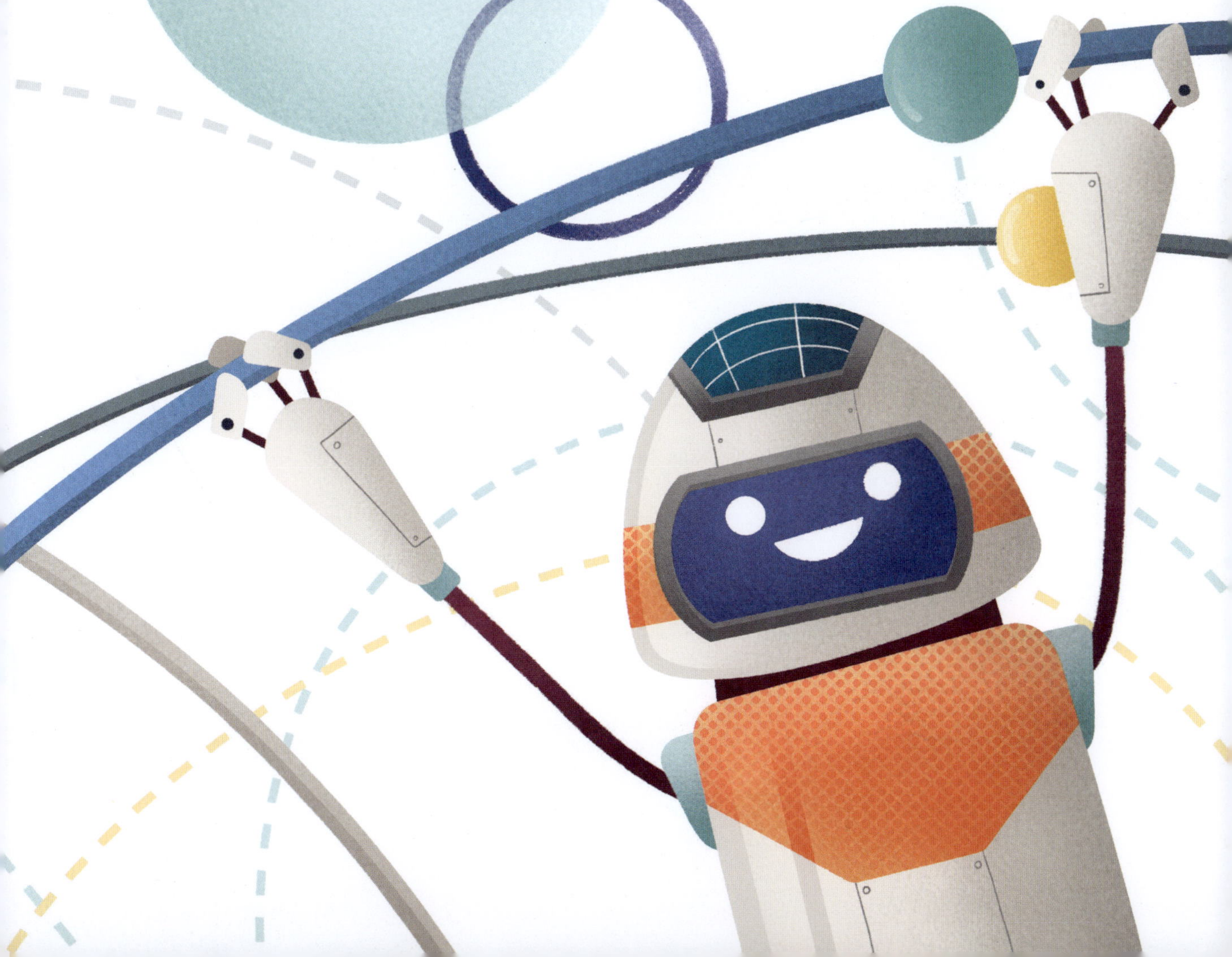

CONTENTS

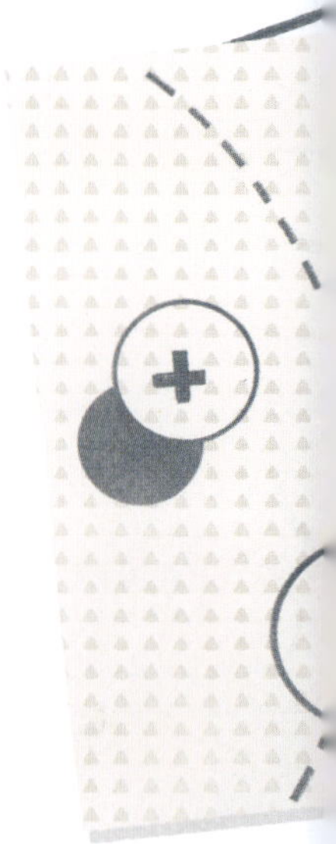

THE SCIENTIFIC METHOD

The **SCIENTIFIC METHOD** is the way in which **SCIENCE** investigates the **REALITY** around us. It is the most reliable method we know to gain **KNOWLEDGE** of things and of the world.

Scientific does not mean "accurate"; instead, it means something is reproducible, that is, it can be repeated. With the same initial conditions, we expect the experiment to always have the same result. The scientific method is experimental, that is, based on experiments, tests, and observations, and this is the fun part in which the scientist becomes creative!

THE MAIN STAGES OF EXPERIMENTAL SCIENTIFIC METHOD ARE:

1. Observing a phenomenon and asking yourself questions.
2. Formulating a hypothesis, that is, a possible explanation of the phenomenon.
3. Carrying out an experiment to check if the hypothesis is correct.
4. Analyzing the results.
5. Repeating the experiment in different ways.
6. Coming to a conclusion and establishing a rule.

TRAVELING WITH YOU!

You can call me **PROF. ALBERT**. I'm a renowned scientist and a lover of outdoor trips and cycling. I'm passionate about life, the universe, and...everything!

They call me **LEO THE SKATER**. I'm a sporty, dynamic guy, and I love comics, doing card tricks like magicians, and playing the guitar. Prof. Albert often asks me to help him with fun experiments.

I'm **GREG** the **ROBOT**, an advanced form of artificial intelligence. I have a positronic brain with too many mistakes in it.

TWO WORDS: SAFETY FIRST!

1. Before doing any experiment, always read all the instructions carefully.

2. It is forbidden to eat or drink during the experiments and, above all, to eat or drink your experiment! It's a bad idea! Don't do it.

3. Use old clothes because you will get dirty! Food coloring can stain your clothing and skin.

4. Wash your hands after every experiment. Some substances you use may be harmful to your health.

Some of the scientific activities in the book require adult supervision.
+

All the words in CAPITAL LETTERS are in the Glossary on pages 46–47, where the terms are explained in more detail.

A SPECIAL FORCE

You undoubtedly have pens, pencils, colored markers, an eraser, a pencil sharpener, and paper clips in your pencil case. Empty everything onto the table and pass a MAGNET over the top. What sticks to it?

A MAGNET attracts only objects containing iron, nickel, or cobalt (FERROMAGNETIC objects), while other objects made of plastic, paper, and wood are not attracted.

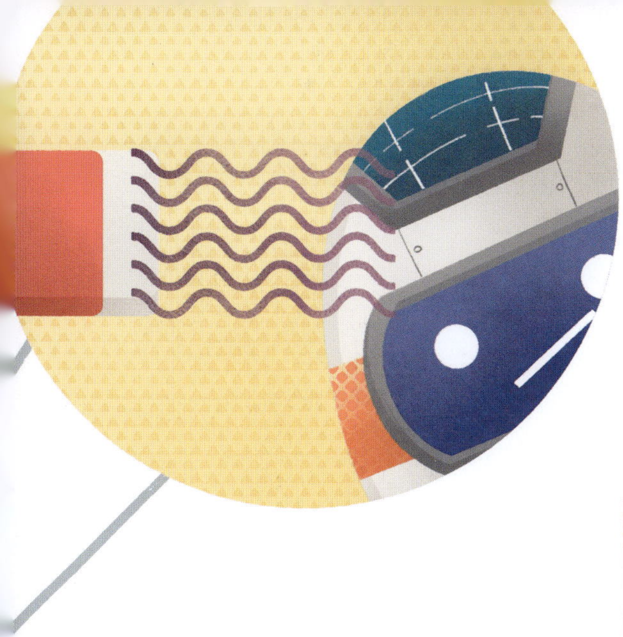

Magnets attract these materials thanks to an invisible force called the MAGNETIC FORCE.

MAGNETIC MUTANTS

Magneto is a character in Marvel Comics. He is a mutant capable of generating and controlling the MAGNETIC FORCE, and therefore he can manipulate metal.

The MAGNETIC FORCE increases if you get closer to the object, and it decreases if you move away from it. It can also pass through different materials such as paper, plastic, and water.

ATTRACTED AND NOT ATTRACTED

YOU WILL NEED

- 1 sheet of colored cardstock
- 1 aluminum tray
- 1 plastic bottle
- 3 paper clips
- 1 magnet
- water
- 1 large bowl
- scissors

DIFFICULTY:

DIRTINESS:

TIME: *10–15 minutes*

DO IT WITH:

HOW TO DO IT

1

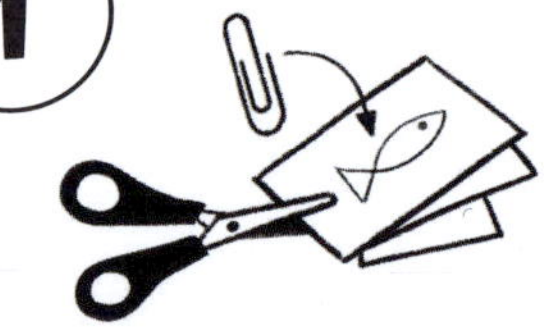

Cut out a fish from the cardstock, the aluminum, and the plastic bottle, then attach a paper clip to each of them.

2

Cut out a second fish from each material.

3

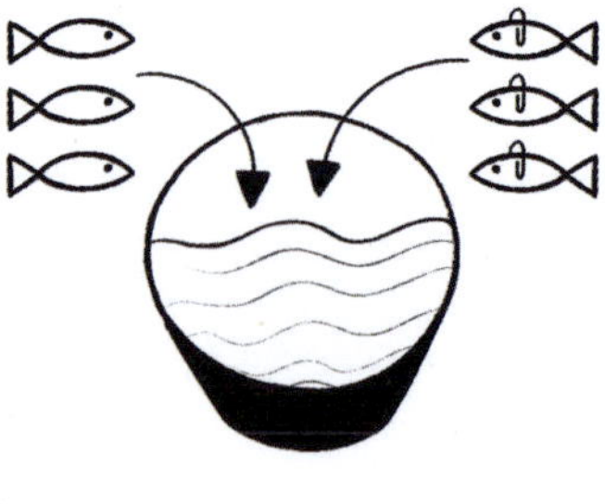

Fill the bowl with water and put all the fish into it.

4

Using the magnet, try to move the fish.

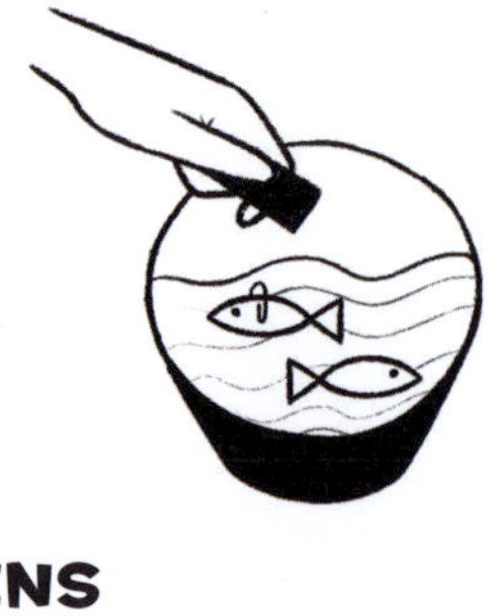

WHAT HAPPENS

The magnet attracts only the plastic, aluminum, and cardstock fish with the paper clips because the clips contain iron, while it doesn't attract the fish without paper clips. The magnetic force also passes through the plastic bowl and the water.

FLYING SPACESHIPS

YOU WILL NEED

- *1 sheet of colored cardstock*
- *1 paper clip*
- *1 magnet*
- *Scotch tape*
- *A piece of thread 8–12 in (20–30 cm) long*

HOW TO DO IT

1 Cut out a spaceship from the piece of cardstock.

2 Tie one end of the thread to a paperclip.

3 Stick the paperclip onto the spaceship with a piece of Scotch tape.

4 Tape the other end of the thread to a table.

5 Use the magnet to make the spaceship fly, without touching the paper clip.

DIFFICULTY:

DIRTINESS:

TIME: *10–15 minutes*

DO IT WITH:

WHAT HAPPENS

The magnetic force pulls the paperclip upwards. If you move the magnet away from the object, the magnetic force decreases and the spaceship falls.

NATURALLY MAGNETIC

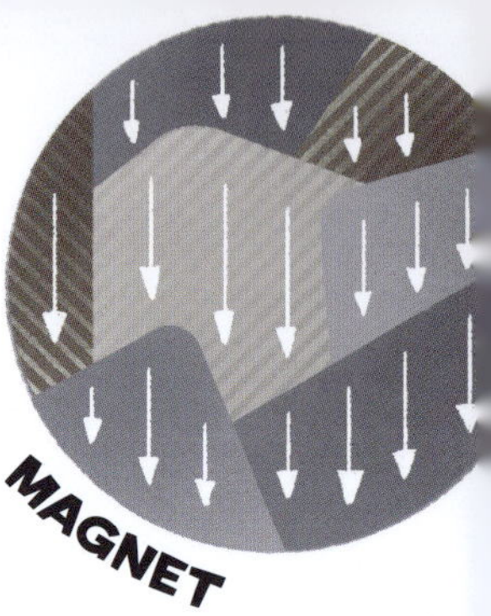

A **magnet** is made of a special mineral called magnetite. The Greeks discovered it more than 2,000 years ago, and its name derives from the city in Turkey where it was found, Magnesia, which is now called Manisa.

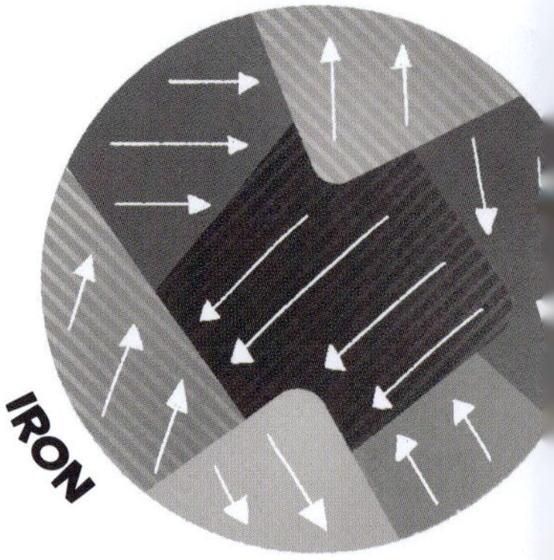

Iron, like all metals, has many **magnetic** areas called DOMAINS, that is, **regions** with uniform magnetization. In magnetite, however, these regions are well-aligned and all point in the same direction.

GETTING ALIGNED!

Magnetite can transfer its power to some metals but not to others. When we put a magnet near a FERROMAGNETIC object, its DOMAINS align and the object becomes a magnet too.

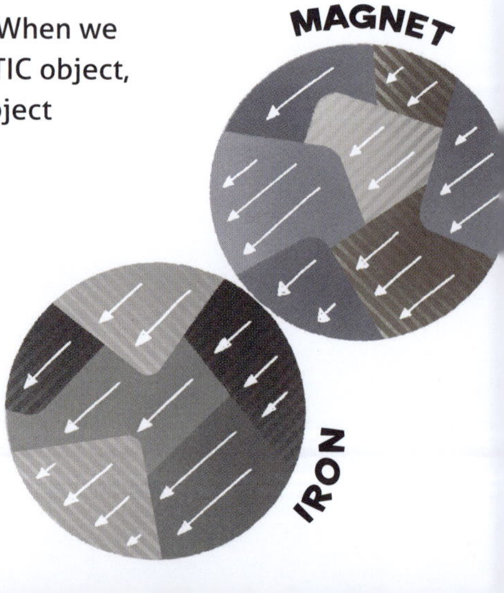

LET'S MAGNETIZE 'EM!

HOW TO DO IT

YOU WILL NEED

- *1 magnet*
- *1 nail*
- *1 sewing needle*

1 Using circular movements, rub the nail over one end of the magnet many times.

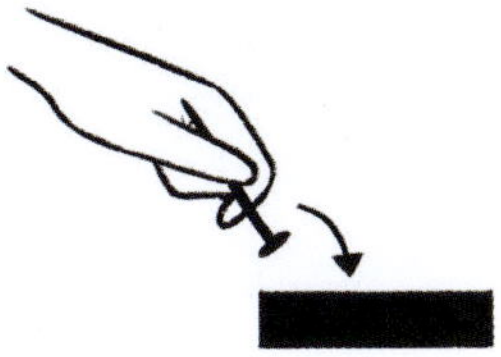

2 Put the nail close to the needle and see what happens.

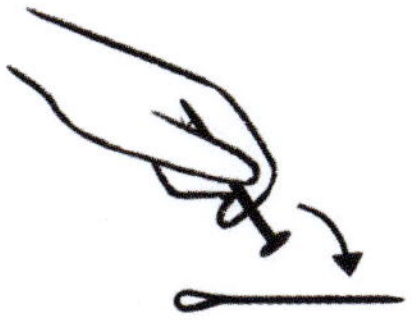

DIFFICULTY:

DIRTINESS:

TIME: *10–15 minutes*

DO IT WITH:

WHAT HAPPENS

When you rub the nail over the magnet it becomes magnetized, causing its magnetic domains to reorient. The nail, which momentarily turns into a magnet, is now able to attract other objects containing iron, such as the needle.

MAGNETIC DRIVE (THE POLES OF A MAGNET)

All magnets have two poles. These are called the **north pole** and the **south pole**.

While one magnet is always attracted to FERROMAGNETIC objects regardless of its orientation, two magnets are only attracted to each other if their opposite poles face each other.

If we put the north pole of one magnet close to the south pole of another, they will attract each other, while if we put two north poles or two south poles close together, the two magnets will repel each other.

DIFFICULTY: 3/5

DIRTINESS: 3/5

TIME: *20 minutes*

DO IT WITH: –

YOU WILL NEED

- *a toy car*
- *2 bar magnets*
- *Scotch tape*
- *2 pieces of red paper and 2 pieces of blue paper*

HOW TO DO IT

1. Position the two magnets so they stick together. On the two ends that are touching each other, attach a piece of red paper on one magnet, and a piece of blue paper on the other, using Scotch tape.

2. Do the same with the other ends, so that each magnet has one red end and one blue end.

Attach one of the magnets to the roof of your car with Scotch tape.

Hold the other magnet close to the car, first one end, then the other. Watch what happens!

WHAT HAPPENS

The forces of magnetic attraction and repulsion between the two magnets makes the toy car move.

TINKERING MACHINE!

Make your toy car with recycled material! You will need 1 plastic bottle, 1 straw, 2 wooden skewers, 4 bottle caps of the same size, Scotch tape, and an awl.

1. Cut the straw into two equal pieces.

2. Glue the two pieces of the straw to the bottle, on the same side, one close to the neck and the other close to the base.

3. Cut the skewers to a length of 4 in (10 cm) and insert them into the straws.

4. With the help of an adult, pierce a hole in the middle of each bottle cap with an awl, then slide them onto the skewers.

YOUR CAR IS READY TO GO!

WE LIVE ON A GIGANTIC MAGNET

THE MAGNETIC FIELD is invisible and is present around a **magnet**.

If we sprinkle iron filings on a **magnet**, they form a circular pattern of MAGNETIC FIELD LINES that go from the top to the bottom of the magnet, revealing the strength of the magnet.

Earth is a gigantic magnet that generates a MAGNETIC FIELD, with MAGNETIC FIELD LINES that connect the poles.

AN AMAZING THING FROM SPACE

Earth's MAGNETIC FIELD protects us from dangerous radiation from the Sun. This protection is weaker at the poles, and so the radioactive particles are able to penetrate the atmosphere there, creating those wonderful beams of light called the aurora borealis, or the northern lights.

SEEING THE INVISIBLE

DIFFICULTY:

DIRTINESS:

TIME: *10 minutes*

DO IT WITH:

YOU WILL NEED

- *syrup*
- *iron filings*
- *1 tablespoon*
- *1 transparent container*
- *1 bar magnet*
- *1 horseshoe magnet*

HOW TO DO IT

1. Mix a glass of syrup with a spoonful of iron filings in the transparent container.

2. Place the bar magnet under the container in different ways and watch what happens.

3. Now try with the horseshoe magnet.

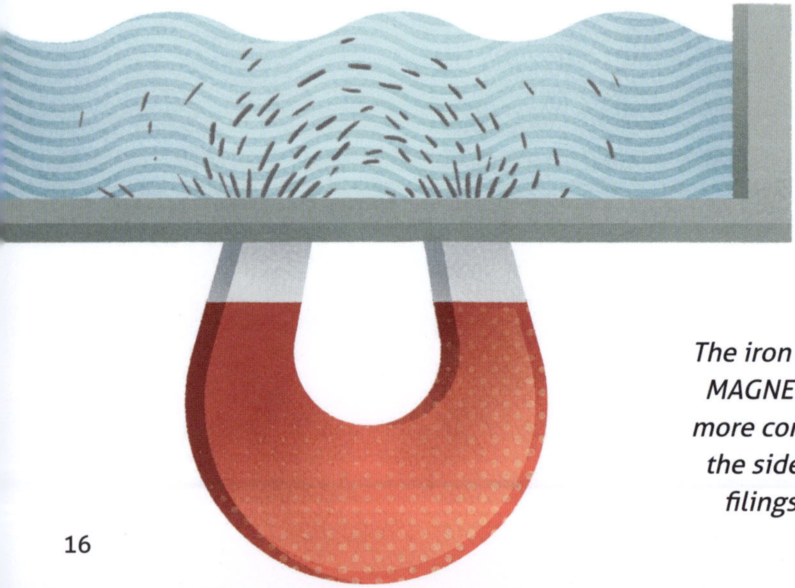

WHAT HAPPENS

The iron filings, attracted by the magnet, all move to the MAGNETIC FIELD LINES of the magnetic field: They are more concentrated at the poles and more widespread at the sides. The syrup slows down the movement of the filings so you can observe the phenomenon better.

LEARN HOW TO USE A COMPASS

YOU WILL NEED

- *1 compass*
- *1 map of your city*

HOW TO DO IT

1

Go outside, put the compass on the ground, and look where it indicates North.

2

Position the map so that North is facing the same way as North on the compass.

3

Look at the streets around you and then at those on the map. Do they correspond?

DIFFICULTY: 1 of 5

DIRTINESS: 1 of 5

TIME: *20 minutes*

DO IT WITH: +

WHAT HAPPENS

Note how the streets on the map correspond exactly to the ones you are looking at.

DID YOU KNOW...

The ancient Romans built cities by orienting the roads with the cardinal points. The two main axes were **THE CARDO** (north-south oriented road) and **THE DECUMANUS** (east-west oriented road).

GET ORIENTED WITH A COMPASS

Many animals, especially migratory ones, are able to orient themselves because of small magnetite crystals in their brains.

Robins, for example, fly miles and miles to return to the same place every winter, and **sea turtles** go back to the same beach where they were born, years later and after having swum across the ocean several times.

DID YOU KNOW...

The invention of the compass is attributed to the Chinese, in around the year 1000. Initially they used it as an attraction and as a tool in rituals. It was only later used as an instrument for navigation.

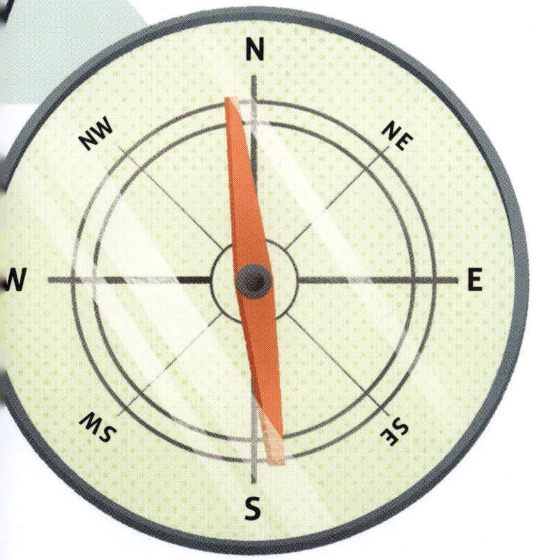

This gentleman is **WILLIAM GILBERT**, and in 1600, thanks to the compass, he was the first person to understand that Earth is a huge magnet!

MAKING A COMPASS

YOU WILL NEED

- *1 cork*
- *1 needle*
- *1 magnet*
- *1 bowl of water*
- *scissors and a knife*
- *Scotch tape*

DIFFICULTY:

DIRTINESS:

TIME: *20 minutes*

DO IT WITH: +

HOW TO DO IT

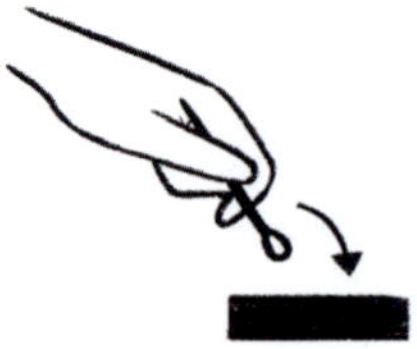

1 Rub the needle over the magnet many times in the same place.

2 Cut a 0.2 in (0.5 cm) wide piece of cork.

3 Attach the needle to the piece of cork with Scotch tape.

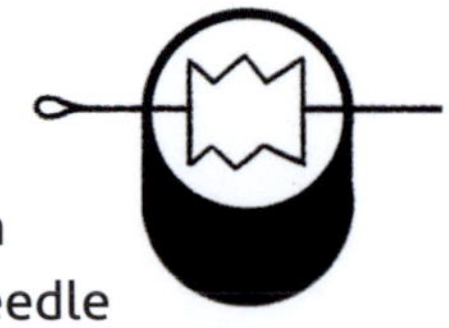

DID YOU KNOW...

Before the compass, sailors oriented themselves by the stars, but this only worked when weather conditions permitted it.
Today we have other more precise and sophisticated tools: satellite navigation systems such as GPS *(Global Positioning System)*.

4 Fill the bowl with water.

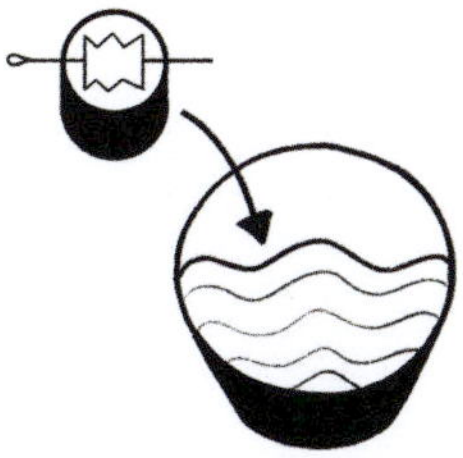

5 Put the cork with the needle on the water.

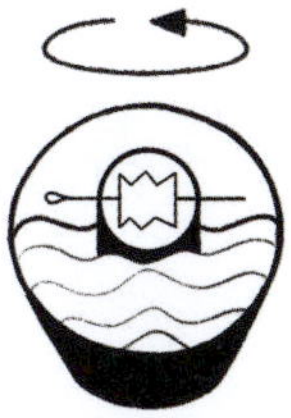

6 Observe how the needle rotates before aligning with Earth's magnetic field.

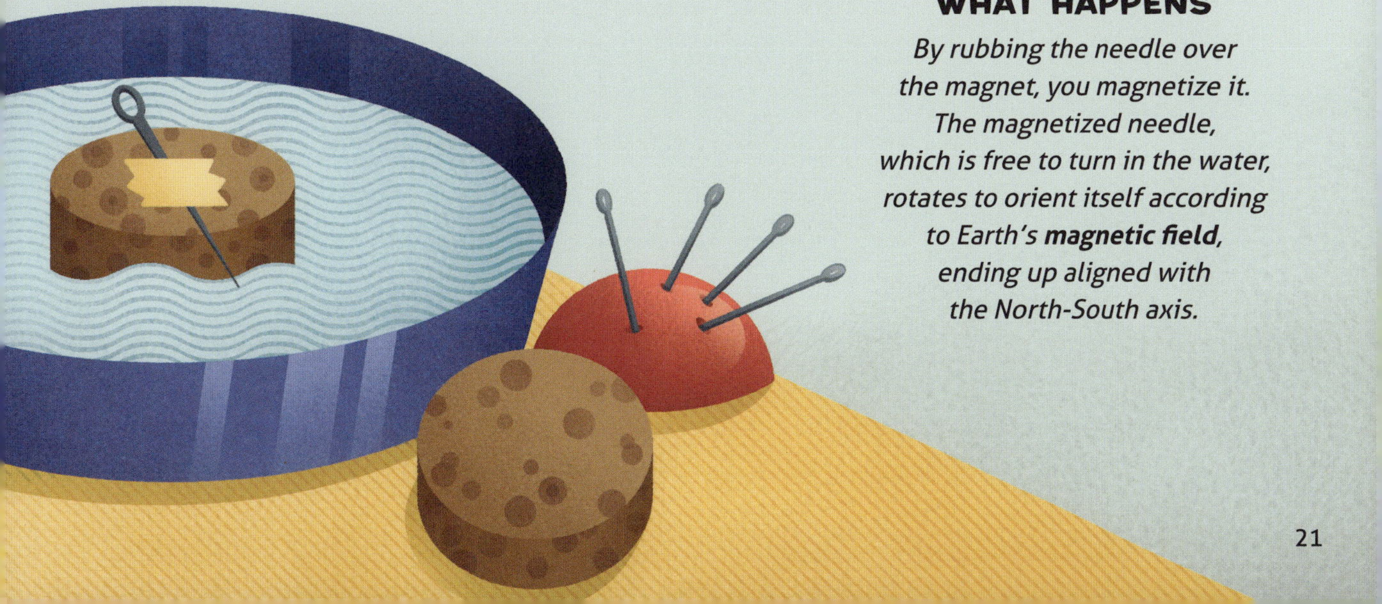

WHAT HAPPENS

By rubbing the needle over the magnet, you magnetize it. The magnetized needle, which is free to turn in the water, rotates to orient itself according to Earth's ***magnetic field****, ending up aligned with the North-South axis.*

USE THE FORCE, LEO

The word "electricity" comes from the Greek word *elektron*, which means **amber**. When amber is rubbed with a cloth, it attracts light objects such as feathers, blades of straw, and threads. This phenomenon is called ELECTROSTATIC **attraction**. There are other materials that can be **electrified** by rubbing, such as glass, rubber, and metals.

ELECTROSTATIC FORCE can be both attractive (attracting objects) and repulsive (repelling objects).

There are two types of ELECTRIC CHARGES: **positive** and **negative**. **Like charges repel each other,** while **opposite charges attract each other.**

AMBER

Normally objects are **neutral**, that is, they contain the same amount of positive and negative particles. When rubbed, however, they are electrified, **becoming positively or negatively charged.**

YOU WILL NEED

- *1 balloon*
- *your hair (!)*
- *a faucet*

DIFFICULTY: 3/5

DIRTINESS: 1/5

TIME: *3 minutes*

DO IT WITH: +

HOW TO DO IT

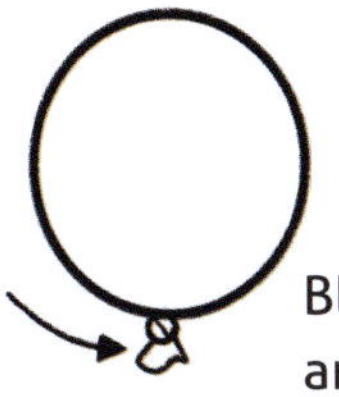

1 Blow up the balloon and tie a knot in it.

2 Rub the balloon over your clean hair.

3 Turn the faucet on so you get a stream of water.

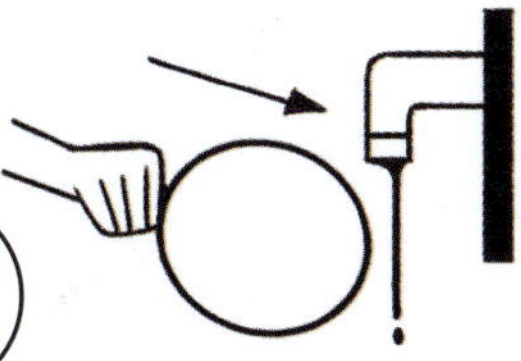

4 Put the balloon near the stream of water and watch what happens.

WHAT HAPPENS

By rubbing the balloon over your hair, it becomes electrically charged. When you put the charged balloon near the water, the water reorients its charges and experiences ELECTROSTATIC attraction, so the stream is deflected.

CAPTURING LIGHTNING

Lightning is a violent electric discharge that forms between the clouds and Earth's surface, or between two nearby clouds when large quantities of opposite CHARGES accumulate.

Scientists have tried to capture the energy of lightning, but they have not had any luck because the energy of lightning is very powerful and very concentrated, and we don't know exactly when and where it will strike.

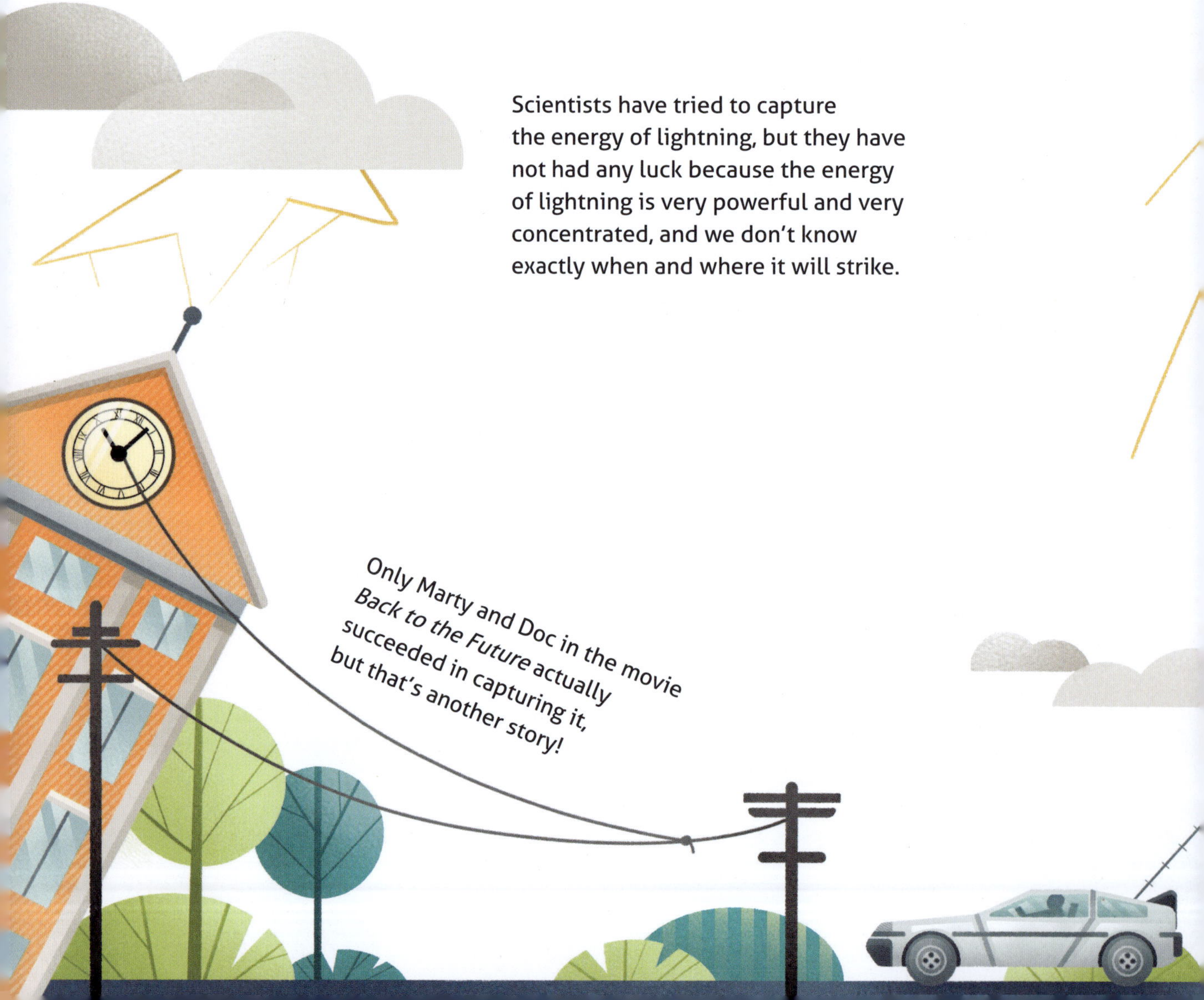

Only Marty and Doc in the movie Back to the Future *actually succeeded in capturing it, but that's another story!*

BENJAMIN FRANKLIN succeeded in deflecting the path of lightning, although he risked his life while doing so. He made a kite with an iron tip and a very long wire. Today's lightning rod was born from his adventure.

NIKOLA TESLA invented an instrument called the Tesla coil, which produces sparks similar to lightning of atmospheric origin, although much less powerful!

THE ELECTROSCOPE

DIFFICULTY: 3/5

DIRTINESS: 3/5

TIME: *30 minutes*

DO IT WITH: +

YOU WILL NEED

- *1 glass jar at least 6 in (15 cm) high, with a plastic lid*
- *4.75 in (12 cm) of stiff metal wire*
- *1 ball of aluminum foil*
- *2 strips of aluminum foil, 1.6 x 0.6 in (4 x 1.5 cm)*
- *1 thumbtack*
- *1 plastic stick*
- *1 wool cloth*
- *Scotch tape*

HOW TO DO IT

1. Make a hole in the lid with the thumbtack.

2. Insert about half of the wire through the hole and secure it with Scotch tape.

3 Slide the aluminum foil ball onto the end of the wire that's sticking out of the top of the lid.

4 Bend the other end of the wire into a small hook and attach the strips of aluminum foil.

5 Put the lid on the jar. Your electroscope is now ready!

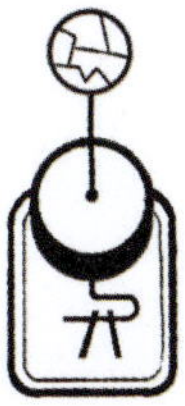

6 Hold the plastic stick close to the aluminum foil ball and watch what happens.

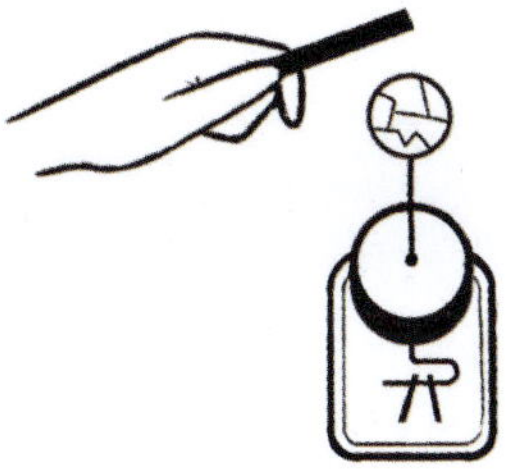

7 Now rub the plastic stick on a wool cloth, hold it close to the aluminum ball, and watch what happens.

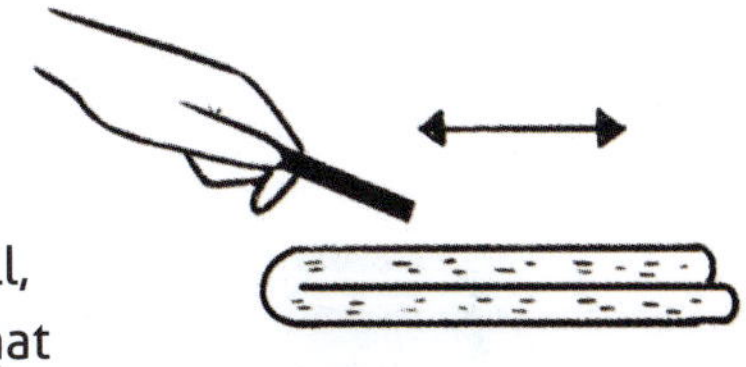

WHAT HAPPENS

When you rub the stick on the cloth it becomes electrified, and when it is held close to the electroscope it transmits the charge to the aluminum foil strips, which repel and move away from each other because they have like charges.

ONCE UPON A TIME, THERE WAS ...

Batteries are devices that produce electricity through a spontaneous chemical reaction that takes place between the substances inside them.

The first electric battery, the forerunner of modern batteries, was invented by **ALESSANDRO VOLTA** around 1800.

Volta's battery was composed of stacked zinc and copper discs, separated by pieces of felt soaked in an acid solution.

FUN FACT

The electric car, which has only recently become popular despite having been invented in the mid-1800s, uses rechargeable batteries instead of fuel to power its engine.

.. THE BATTERY

DIFFICULTY:

DIRTINESS:

TIME: *30 minutes*

DO IT WITH:

YOU WILL NEED

- *8 dimes*
- *a sheet of paper*
- *a sheet of aluminum foil*
- *scissors*
- *a glass*
- *1 lemon*
- *a teaspoon*
- *a small LED light*

HOW TO DO IT

1. Use a dime to draw and cut out 8 discs of paper and 8 discs of aluminum foil.

2. Wet the paper discs with a little lemon juice.

3. Stack the discs in the following order: coin, lemon-soaked paper, and aluminum foil, and continue with this pattern.

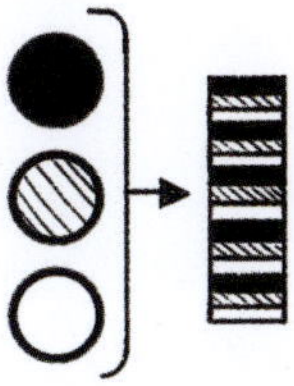

4. Attach the LED light to the ends of the battery.

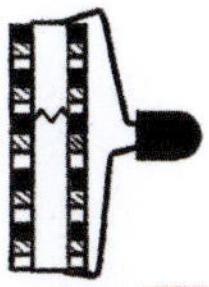

WARNING!

Try not to let the lemon juice on the paper discs drip down the battery, as it could create a short circuit, and the LED light won't light up!

WHAT HAPPENS

Thanks to the acid solution between zinc and copper, electrons pass through the battery. The more stacked sets of the three discs, the more powerful the battery will be.

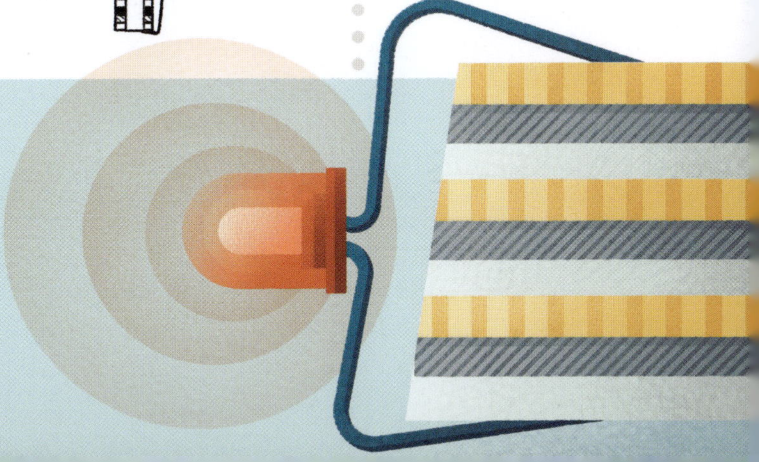

ELECTRICITY...

The term "current"comes from the Latin *currens*, which means "running." It is used to indicate the flow of electrons moving from one area to another, accelerated through an imbalance of charge called POTENTIAL DIFFERENCE. This is measured in volts, in honor of **ALESSANDRO VOLTA**.

V

VOLT

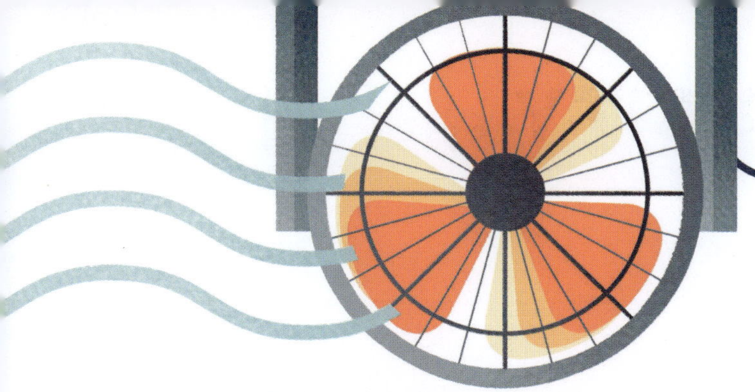

... IN EVERYDAY LIFE

Today, the electrical systems in our homes use **alternating current** (AC), which was designed by **NIKOLA TESLA**. It is better and more practical than the **direct current** (DC) promoted by **THOMAS EDISON**, which today we use almost exclusively for **batteries**.

LET'S BUILD A CIRCUIT

An ELECTRIC CIRCUIT is an unbroken path through which electrons can flow.

The simplest circuit is made up of:

- A **generator** or **battery**, that is, a device that converts other energy sources into electricity.
- An **electrical device**. For example, a light bulb, a fan, or an iron.
- **Wire conductors** that connect all the elements of the circuit, allowing the current to flow easily through it.

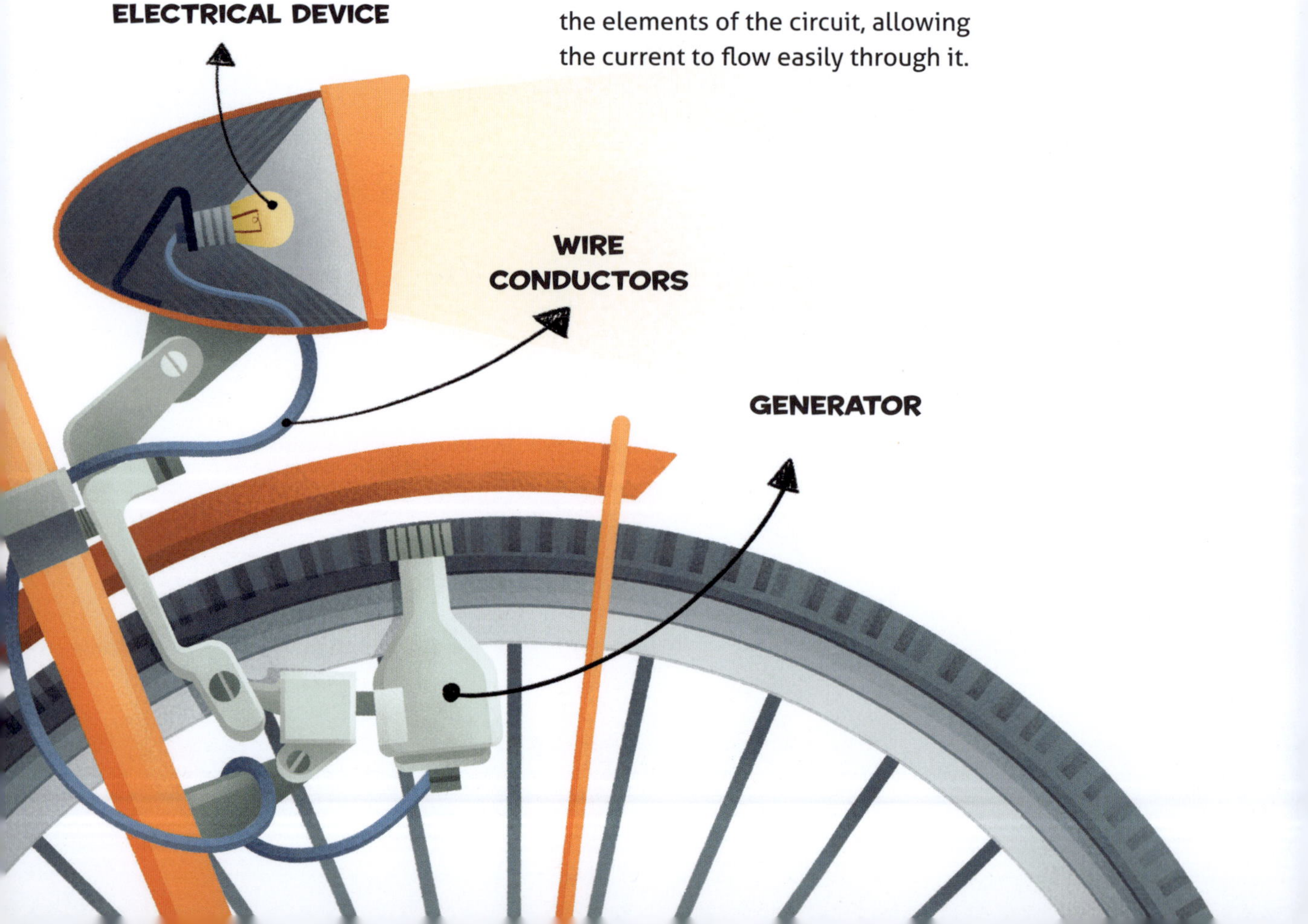

YOU WILL NEED

- *bare electrical wire*
- *4.5-volt battery*
- *4.5-volt light bulb*
- *light bulb holder*
- *scissors*

HOW TO DO IT

DIFFICULTY: 3 of 5

DIRTINESS: 2 of 5

TIME: *30 minutes*

DO IT WITH: +

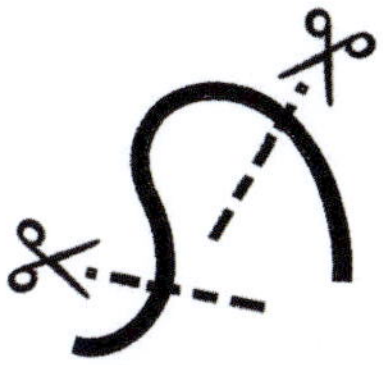

1 Cut 2 pieces of electrical wire, each 8 in (20 cm) long.

2 Connect one end of each of the wires to one of the battery poles, being careful not to let the two wires touch each other.

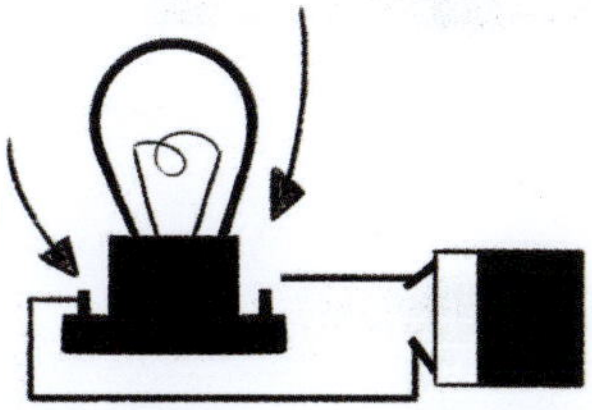

3 Put the light bulb in the holder and connect the two free ends of the wires to the holder.

4 Watch what happens.

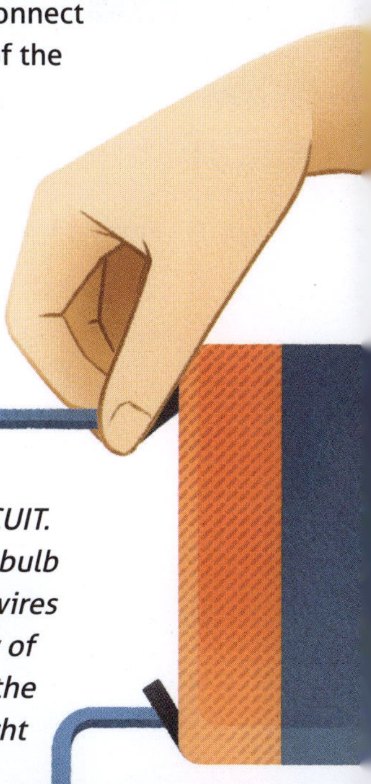

WHAT HAPPENS

You have built an ELECTRIC CIRCUIT. The battery is the generator, the bulb is the electrical device, and the wires are the connection for the flow of ELECTRIC CURRENT. Thanks to the flow of electric current, the light bulb turns on!

CONDUCTORS AND INSULATORS

Not all materials allow electric current to pass through them; some materials have high electron mobility, while others don't.

Metals like iron, copper, and aluminum are CONDUCTORS that allow ELECTRIC CURRENT to pass through them.

Other materials, however, such as wood, glass, and plastic do not allow ELECTRIC CURRENT to pass through them. These materials are called INSULATORS.

DOES WATER CONDUCT ELECTRICITY OR NOT?

Tap water, rainwater, seawater, and river water contain dissolved substances that allow them to become good CONDUCTORS. But be careful! Pure water, also called distilled water, doesn't contain any dissolved substances and therefore doesn't conduct ELECTRIC CURRENT.

IT CONDUCTS!

YOU WILL NEED

• the electric circuit you made previously
• pieces of or objects made of different materials, for example, wood (clothes pin), plastic (marker lid), fabric (or wool yarn), paper, aluminum, iron (nail), rubber, elastic, copper wire
• piece of paper and a pencil

DIFFICULTY: 3/5

DIRTINESS: 2/5

TIME: *30 minutes*

DO IT WITH: +

HOW TO DO IT

1. Cut one of the electrical wires in half.

2. Insert one of the objects you have chosen between the two ends of the cut wire. Make sure the wires are fully touching the object.

3. Now try the other materials, one at a time.

4. Make a note of which materials light up the bulb.

WHAT HAPPENS

The bulb lights up with some materials, such as aluminum, copper, and iron, because they are good conductors. It does not light up with other materials, such as paper, plastic, or rubber, because they are insulators.

SOFT CIRCUITS

DIFFICULTY:

DIRTINESS:

TIME: *1 hour*

DO IT WITH:

+

YOU WILL NEED

- *conductive dough (see recipe)*
- *non-conductive dough (see recipe)*
- *1 small LED light*
- *2 bare electrical wires*
- *4.5 volt battery*
- *Scotch tape*

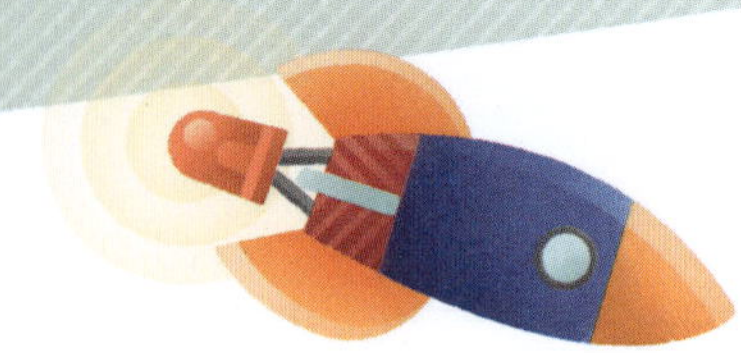

RECIPE FOR CONDUCTIVE DOUGH

4/5 cup (200 ml) water
2 cups (210 g) flour
6 Tbsp (90 g) salt
3/5 cup (130 ml) lemon juice
1 Tbsp vegetable oil
1 Tbsp powdered food coloring

Put the water, 1 3/5 cups (160 g) of flour, the salt, lemon juice, and oil in a saucepan. Mix thoroughly, then cook over moderate heat until you get a ball of modeling dough. Leave to cool on a baking pan for a few minutes. Add the rest of the flour and the food coloring, then hand knead the dough thoroughly. Your conductive modeling dough is now ready.

RECIPE FOR NON-CONDUCTIVE DOUGH

2/5 cup (80 g) sugar
1 1/2 cups (140 g) flour
About 4/5 cup (200 ml) distilled water
3 tbsp vegetable oil

Put half the flour, all the sugar, and the oil in a bowl, then mix thoroughly. Add a teaspoon of distilled water at a time, followed by the remaining flour, then knead the dough thoroughly. It's now ready!

You can keep both doughs wrapped in plastic wrap in an airtight container for several weeks.

1. Make the two doughs following the recipes.

2. Make 2 rolls of conductive dough; they will be your conductors, but do not let them touch each other.

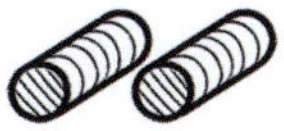

3. Attach one end of each wire to one of the battery's poles and secure them with Scotch tape.

4. Insert the other two ends into the two rolls of conductive dough.

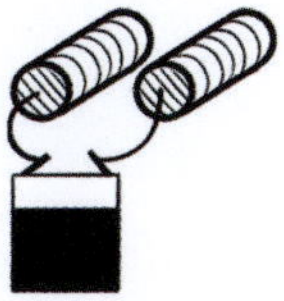

5. Insert the legs of the LED light into the rolls of dough, making sure that the longest leg is in the roll connected to the positive pole of the battery. The LED light will light up.

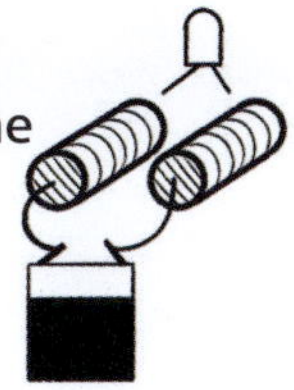

6. Briefly touch the rolls with a new piece of dough and then remove it. What do you notice?

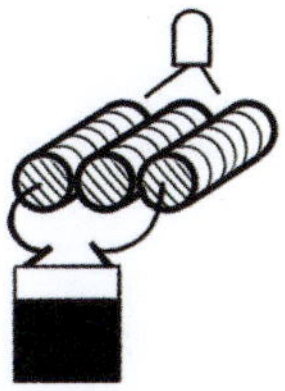

7. Now put a piece of non-conductive dough between the two rolls. What happens?

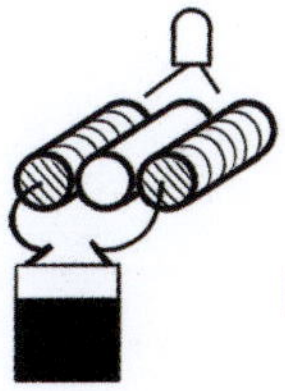

WHAT HAPPENS

If you put the two rolls of conductive dough so they touch each other, a short circuit is created. The current chooses the shortest route and passes through the contact point without going through the LED light, which therefore does not light up. If you put a piece of non-conductive dough between the two rolls of conductive dough, it acts as an insulator, so the electric current will pass through the LED light, which then lights up. Once you have finished your circuit, you can play with the remaining conductive dough, letting your imagination run wild to create lots of fun shapes.

THE ADVENT OF ELECTROMAGNETISM

AMPÈRE AND ØRSTED

Up until the early nineteenth century, it was thought that magnetism and electricity were two completely different phenomena. The scientists Ampère and Ørsted were the first to imagine that these two forces were very closely linked. They demonstrated that an ELECTRIC FIELD can generate a MAGNETIC FIELD, and in the same period, Faraday demonstrated that a MAGNETIC FIELD can also generate an ELECTRIC FIELD.

These studies were the start of an unimaginable technological revolution—ELECTROMAGNETISM—which led to an incredible series of inventions!

Like in any great technological or scientific revolution, inventions didn't appear suddenly. They were the result of the contributions and collaboration of many different scientists, such as Samuel Morse, Thomas Edison, Nikola Tesla, Guglielmo Marconi, and many others.

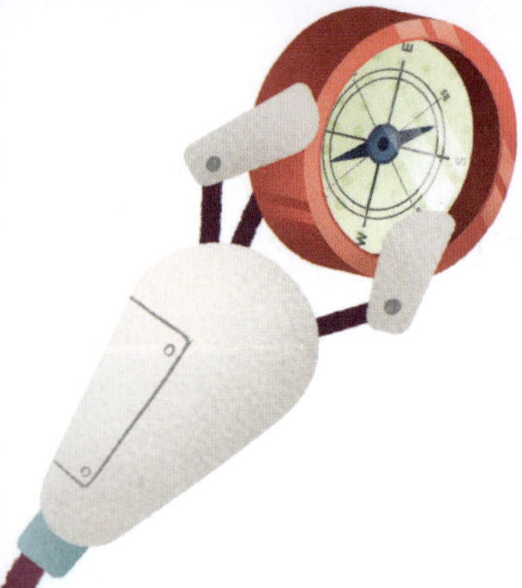

A CELL PHONE AND A COMPASS

YOU WILL NEED

- *a compass*
- *a cell phone*

DIFFICULTY: 5/5

DIRTINESS: 1/5

TIME: *20 minutes*

DO IT WITH: + adult

HOW TO DO IT

1 Pass the cell phone over the compass and watch what happens carefully.

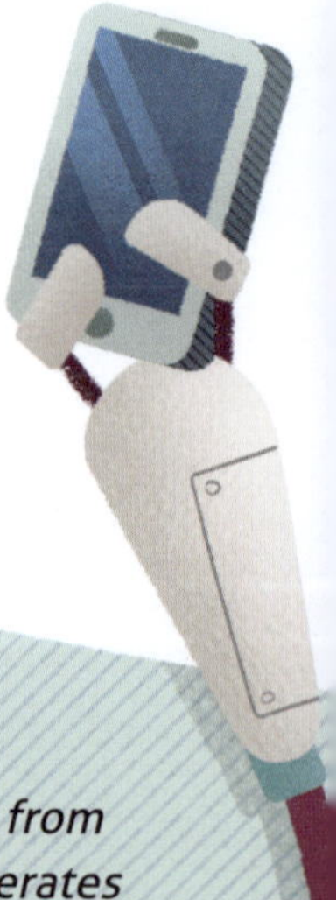

WHAT HAPPENS

The cell phone uses the electricity from its battery. The electric current generates a magnetic field that can be detected by the moving compass needle.

A MAGNET AND A COIL

DIFFICULTY:

DIRTINESS:

TIME: *20 minutes*

DO IT WITH:

YOU WILL NEED

- *1 tester*
- *1 bar magnet*
- *1 coated copper wire (winding wire) long enough to wind around the magnet 50 times*
- *1 piece of corrugated cardboard*
- *scissors*
- *glue*

HOW TO DO IT

1

Using scissors, glue, and cardboard, make a block that is slightly larger than the magnet.

2

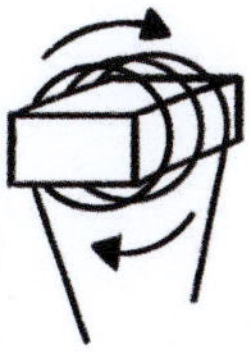

Wrap the copper wire around the cardboard block 50 times to make a coil.

3

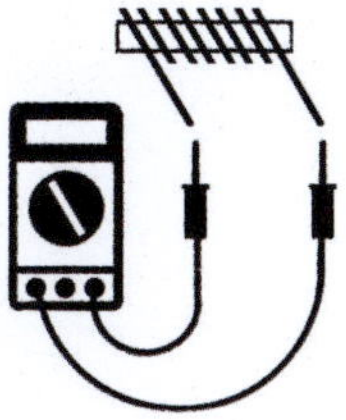

Attach the ends of the copper wire to the tester.

4

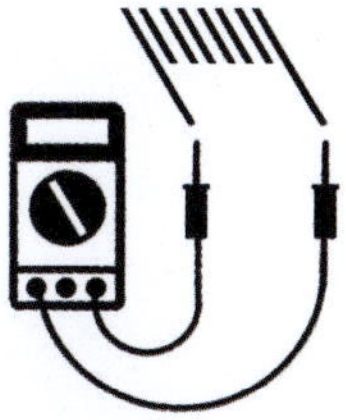

Remove the cardboard block from the coil and insert the magnet in its place.

5

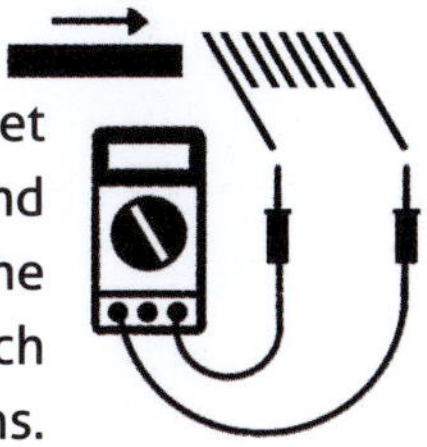

Move the magnet backward and forward inside the coil and watch what happens.

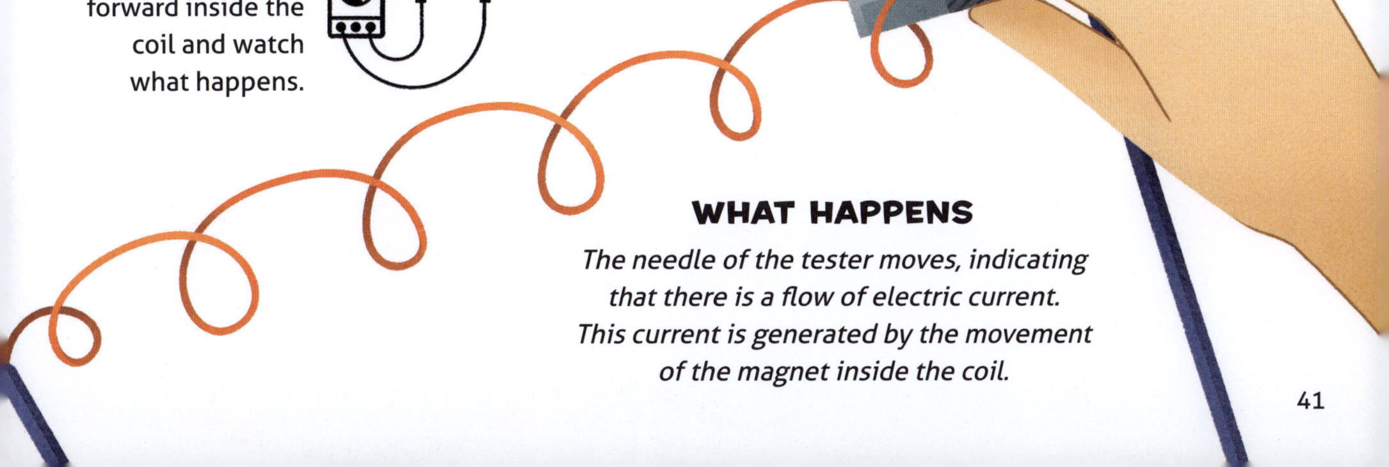

WHAT HAPPENS

The needle of the tester moves, indicating that there is a flow of electric current. This current is generated by the movement of the magnet inside the coil.

A SIMPLE ELECTRIC MOTOR

Appliances such as blenders, washing machines, dishwashers, and hair dryers, but also cars and forms of public transportation, use an **electric motor** to transform **electrical energy** into **mechanical energy**.

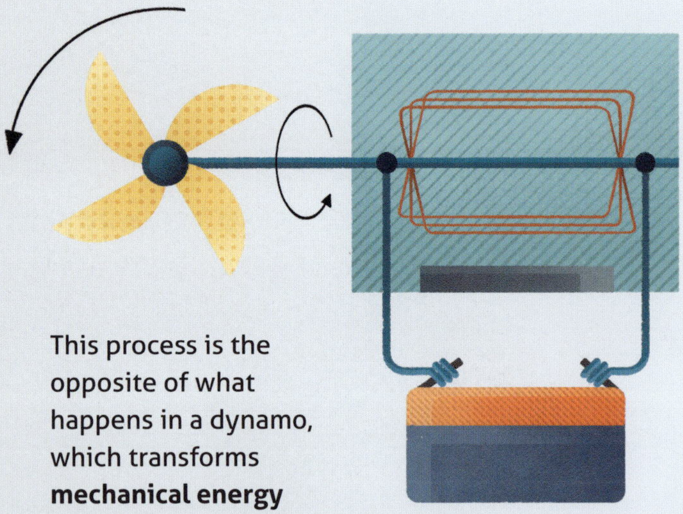

This process is the opposite of what happens in a dynamo, which transforms **mechanical energy** into **electrical energy**.

YOU WILL NEED

- *1 button magnet*
- *1 piece of styrofoam, 4 x 4 in (10 x 10 cr*
- *2 large paper clips*
- *3.3 ft (1 meter) of coated copper wire (enameled winding wire)*
- *2 x 4 in (10 cm) long pieces of bare electrical wire*
- *1.5 volt battery*
- *scissors*
- *Scotch tape*

HOW TO DO IT

1. Attach the magnet to the middle of the styrofoam with Scotch tape.

2. Wrap the coated copper wire around itself, so as to make a ring with lots of coils.

3. 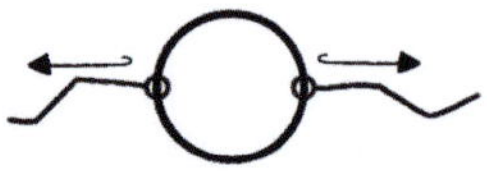

Leave 2 in (5 cm) of wire free at each end.

DIFFICULTY: 5 of 5

DIRTINESS: 3 of 5

TIME: *20 minutes*

DO IT WITH: +

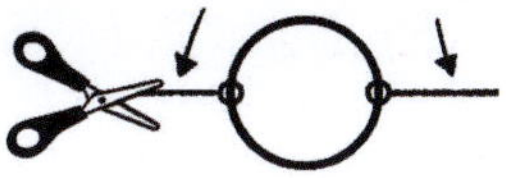

4 Straighten the ends of the wire and scrape off the coating on the top side of the wire with scissors.

5 Make the supports for the coil by opening both the paper clips to form a *P* shape.

6 Now insert the supports into the styrofoam, one on the left of the magnet, and the other on the right.

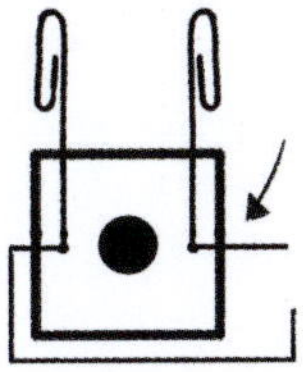

7 Attach the two electrical wires to the bottom of the two paper clips.

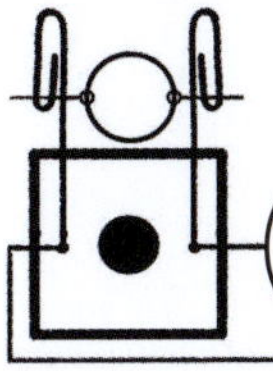

8 Insert the ends of the coil into the rings in the supports, this way the coil can turn freely.

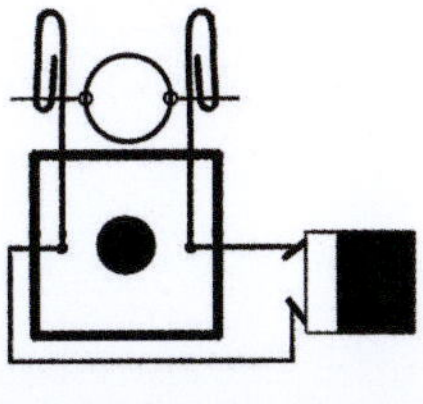

9 Attach the free ends of the electrical wire to the battery with Scotch tape, then push the coil so it starts to turn.

WARNING!

This experiment can cause both the coil and the battery to get hot.

WHAT HAPPENS

The coil starts to turn because part of the copper wire ends is a conductor and part is an insulator. This means there is an alternating flow of current, and consequently it will produce an intermittent magnetic field that interacts with the underlying magnet.

NO TOUCHING

The aim of this experiment is to not touch the wire with the loop, so as to avoid closing the circuit.

DIFFICULTY:

DIRTINESS:

TIME: *30 minutes*

DO IT WITH:

HOW TO DO IT

YOU WILL NEED

- *cardboard*
- *styrofoam*
- *hot glue*
- *Scotch tape and double-sided tape*
- *button magnet with a diameter of 0.2 in (6 mm) and height of 0.1 in (3 mm)*
- *2 in (5 cm) bar magnet*
- *5 ft (1.5 meters) iron wire with a diameter of 0.07 in (2 mm)*
- *bare electrical wire*
- *buzzer*
- *4.5 volt battery*
- *wooden skewer*
- *pencil*
- *plastic casing of a ballpoint pen*
- *paper clip with a diameter of 0.8 in (2 cm) made into a hook shape*

1

Cut out two 8 x 16 in (20 x 40 cm) cardboard and styrofoam rectangles. Stick them together with double-sided tape.

2

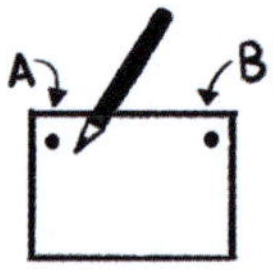

Draw two circles on the cardboard side to mark points A and B.

3

Insert the wire into point B, piercing both the cardboard and the styrofoam, and fix in place with glue.

4

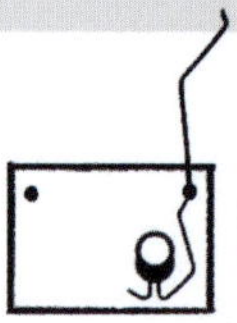

Attach the black wire of the buzzer to the iron wire at point B.

5

Bend the iron wire however you like to create lots of curves.

6

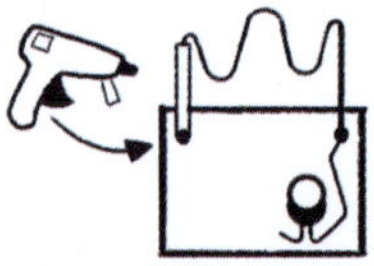

Insert the end of the iron wire into the casing of the ballpoint pen. Insert both the casing and the wire into point A, piercing both the cardboard and the styrofoam, then fix in place with glue.

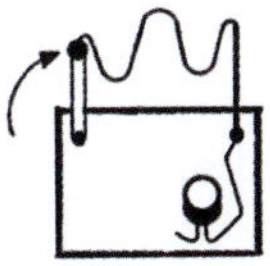

7

Put the button magnet anywhere you like along the iron wire.

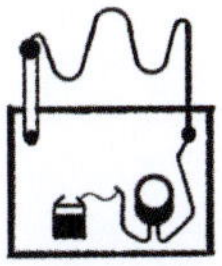

8

Attach the red wire of the buzzer to the positive pole of the battery.

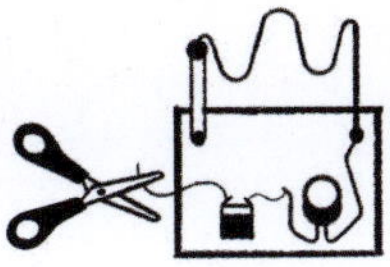

9

Cut 24 in (60 cm) of bare electrical wire and attach it to the negative pole of the battery.

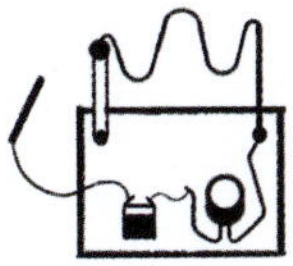

10

Attach the electrical wire to the wooden skewer with Scotch tape.

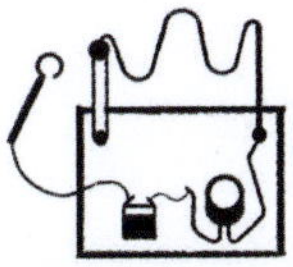

11

Connect the hook-shaped paperclip to the electrical wire at the bottom of the skewer using Scotch tape.

12

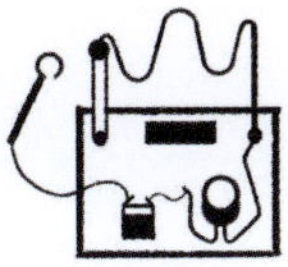

Use the hot glue to stick the bar magnet underneath one of the curves in the iron wire, at a distance of 0.4 in (1 cm); you can make the magnet higher by sticking a few pieces of cardboard together underneath it.

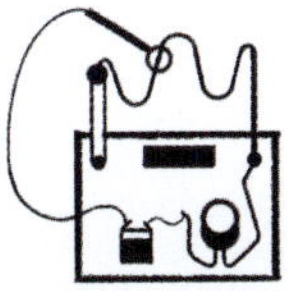

13

Hook the hook onto the ballpoint pen casing and close it to form a loop, maintaining a diameter of 0.8 in (2 cm). You can now start playing!

You can use a small light bulb instead of a buzzer!

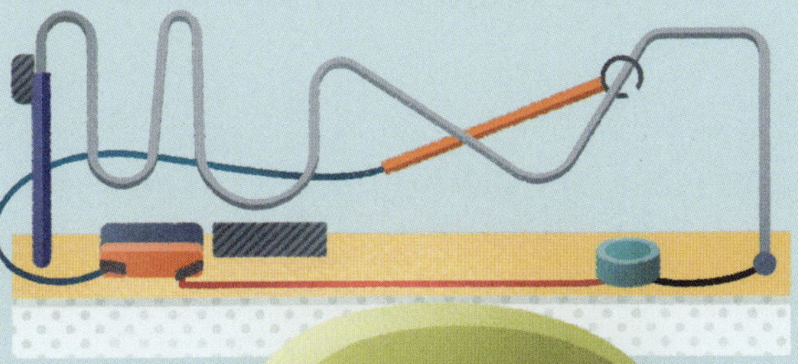

WHAT HAPPENS

When the loop touches the iron wire the circuit closes, allowing the electric charges to pass through and buzz the buzzer. To make it even more complicated, the two magnets attract the loop.

GLOSSARY

CONDUCTOR (ELECTRIC): A material through which electricity can flow easily.

DOMAIN: The region of a ferromagnetic material with uniform magnetization.

ELECTRIC CHARGE: A property of matter that controls how particles are affected by an electric or magnetic field. It can be positive or negative; like charges repel each other, and opposite charges attract each other.

ELECTRIC CIRCUIT: A closed path through which electric current flows.

ELECTRIC CURRENT: The flow of electrons inside a conductor. With direct current the current is constant and always flows in the same direction. With alternating current the current changes over time and reverses direction.

ELECTRIC FIELD: The area surrounding electric charges.

ELECTROMAGNETISM: The relationship between electric and magnetic phenomena.

ELECTROSTATIC FORCE: The attractive or repulsive force between two electrically charged objects.

FERROMAGNETIC: Describes material such as iron, nickel, or cobalt that is attracted to a magnet and assumes its properties (becoming magnetized).

INSULATOR (ELECTRIC): A material that does not allow electricity to pass easily through it.

MAGNET: A body capable of attracting ferromagnetic materials.

MAGNETIC FIELD: Area surrounding magnetic charges.

MAGNETIC FIELD LINES (OF THE MAGNETIC FIELD): Invisible lines that represent the distribution and direction of the force generated by the magnetic field in the presence of a magnetic charge. In the magnetic field, each line indicates the direction a magnet would point if placed at that location. The lines have an orientation, that is, a direction.

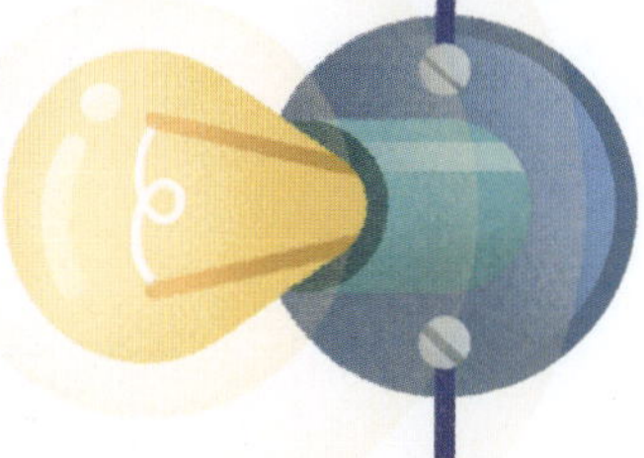

MAGNETIC FORCE: The force of attraction or repulsion between magnetic charges; the ability of a magnet to attract ferromagnetic materials.

POTENTIAL DIFFERENCE: The difference in electrical potential between two points.

VALERIA BARATTINI

Valeria holds a master's degree in Economics and Management of Arts and Cultural Activities from the University of Ca' Foscari in Venice, and a master's in Standards for Museum Education from the Roma Tre University. She works in education and cultural planning. Since 2015, she has been working in partnership with Fosforo, holding events and activities in the field of scientific dissemination and informal teaching.

MATTIA CRIVELLINI

A graduate of Computer Science at the University of Bologna, Mattia has been studying Cognitive Sciences in the United States at Indiana University. Since 2011, he has been the director of Fosforo, the science festival of Senigallia. He organizes and plans activities, conferences, and shows for communication and dissemination of science in Italy and abroad through the NEXT Cultural Association.

ALESSANDRO GNUCCI

A science communicator and tutor, with over fifteen years of experience. In 2011, he founded Fosforo, the science festival in Senigallia, and in 2014, the Cultural Association NEXT. He designs science communication formats, and organises shows together with his colleagues at the PSIQUADRO association.

FRANCESCA GORINI

After obtaining a master's degree in Industrial Biotechnology from the University of Urbino "Carlo Bo" and doing an internship in Cambridge (UK), Francesca obtained a PhD in Molecular Medicine at the Vita Salute San Raffaele University in Milan. She has dedicated herself to research in various laboratories and to the management of clinical studies in hospitals. She teaches in schools and collaborates with Fosforo in scientific dissemination.

ROSSELLA TRIONFETTI

After graduating in Applied Arts, Rossella specialized in the field of illustration and graphics by attending various courses with professionals in the sector, including at the Mimaster of Milan. Currently, she works as an illustrator of children's books and also collaborates in the creation of apps. In recent years, she has illustrated several books for White Star Kids.

Valeria, Mattia, Alessandro, Francesca and Rossella are all part of

FOSFORO: THE SCIENCE FESTIVAL.

Fosforo: It's a fair, a festival, a meeting place. It's a series of events to give stimuli, overturn the commonplace, make people fall in love with science, and stimulate them to dream, think, invent, and discover. Fosforo: It's scientific dissemination. An event with national and international guests, who, since 2011, have been animating Senigallia, in the Marche region of Italy, for four days in May. This is done with surprising scientific exhibitions, laboratories, and conferences on the main scientific topics.

WHITE STAR KIDS

White Star Kids™ is a trademark of White Star s.r.l.

Piazzale Luigi Cadorna, 6
20123 Milan, Italy
www.whitestar.it

Translation: TperTradurre, Rome, Italy
Editing: Michele Suchomel-Casey

ISBN 978-88-544-1729-8
2 3 4 5 6   28 27 26 25 24

Printed in China

MIX
Paper from responsible sources
FSC www.fsc.org
FSC® C178000